Nancy Patricia Pelosi is an American politician who currently serves as the Minority Leader of the United States House of Representatives, representing California's 12th congressional district. She previously served as the 52nd House Speaker from 2007 to 2011, the only woman to do so. As Speaker, she attained the highest rank of any female politician in American history.

A member of the Democratic Party, Pelosi represents California's 12th congressional district, which consists of four-fifths of the city and county of San Francisco.

She served as the House Minority Whip from 2002 to 2003, and was House Minority Leader from 2003 to 2007.

 Pelosi is the first woman, the first Californian, and first Italian-American to lead a major party in Congress. After the Democrats took control of the House in 2007 and increased their majority in 2009.

On November 17, 2010, Pelosi was elected as the Democratic Leader by House Democrats and therefore the Minority Leader in the Republican-controlled House for the 112th Congress.

All In The Family:

A History of Corruption and Protection

According to World Biography, 2017, *Nancy Pelosi began her career in politics at a young age. Her father, Thomas "Tommy" J. D'Alesandro Jr., was a popular local politician from the Little Italy section of Baltimore, Maryland. Just a year before Pelosi was born, her father won election to the same U.S. House of Representatives in which she would serve many years later.*

Pelosi's father was well-known in Little Italy, and went on to become a Baltimore legend. When she was seven years old, he became the city's first Italian-American mayor. He served three terms, and so Pelosi was known as the mayor's daughter for most of her childhood and teens.

Thomas D'Alesandro Jr.'s political career was not without controversy. There had long been speculation about the extent of D'Alesandro's connection to the Mafia. The concern reached the highest levels of government with John F Kennedy questioning whether he could trust D'Alesandro, Attorney General Robert Kennedy commenced an investigation led by FBI Director, J. Edgar Hoover. The files have only recently been released.

(Thomas D'Alesandro Jr.)

According to Thorn, Victor, 2010, *D'Alessandro served in U.S. military intelligence during WWII, whereupon, according to veteran reporter Wayne Madsen, on Sept. 25, 2006, he "broadcast wartime radio messages to Italy exhorting Italians to rise up against Benito Mussolini."*

On the surface, such an endeavor sounds commendable. But another participant in this operation was imprisoned gangster Lucky Luciano, who cut a deal with the feds. In return for convincing Sicilian Mafioso to assist the Navy in their war efforts, they would deport him back to Italy.

Once free, Luciano teamed up with Jewish crime kingpin Meyer Lansky; and as Alfred W. McCoy relates in The Politics of Heroin in Southeast Asia, they began trafficking the drug into the United States. One of the primary entry spots used during this time was at Baltimore, which Mrs. Pelosi's father oversaw after becoming mayor of the city in 1947.

(Lucky Luciano)

According to Crawford, Phillip, 2015, *Nancy Pelosi's father, Thomas D'Alesandro Jr. allegedly was a constant companion of notorious mobster Benjamin "Benny Trotta" Magliano and other underworld figures during his political years in Baltimore, MD. D'Alesandro was a Congressman for five terms from 1938 to 1947, and Baltimore mayor for three terms from 1947 to 1959. Magliano was identified by the FBI as one of Baltimore's "top hoodlums," and he widely was acknowledged as the representative for New York's Frankie Carbo who made his bones with Murder, Inc. and later became a made guy in the Lucchese family. The allegations are included in D'Alesandro's recently-released FBI files which Friends of Ours has obtained pursuant to the Freedom of Information Act.*

In 1947 the FBI investigated Magliano for securing a draft exemption from Selective Service for himself and prize fighters he controlled by falsely representing they had essential employment at American Ship Cleaning Company which was operated by John Cataneo. In fact, Magliano and his boxers had no such employment, and they were convicted with Cataneo in federal court for their unpatriotic draft-dodging scam. Peter Galiano, one of the convicted boxers, told the FBI in January 1947 that "Thomas D'Alesandro was a constant companion of John Cataneo and Benjamin Magliano.

It was reported that these individuals had worked hard for Thomas D'Alesandro's reelection to Congress and on his campaign at that time to become Mayor of Baltimore. It was stated that John Cataneo and Magliano during the time of this campaign were under Federal indictments for violation of the Selective Service Act and for fraud against the Government and were subsequently convicted in Federal court. Cataneo allegedly admitted giving large sums of money toward the Democratic campaign and stated that he would receive the sanitation contracts for Baltimore if Mr. D'Alesandro was elected mayor.

At that time the FBI never investigated D'Alesandro concerning this or numerous other allegations involving hoodlum associations and public corruption. Of course, while in Congress D'Alesandro sat on the appropriations committee and was a friend of Director J. Edgar Hoover. For example, an FBI memo dated March 27, 1946 from E. G. Fitch to D. M. Ladd provides:

Supervisor Orrin H. Bartlett advised me that while talking to Congressman Thomas D'Alesandro, Jr. on March 26, 1946, the Congressman advised Agent Bartlett he was running for Congress again in the fall 1946 election and that in 1947 he was running for the office of Mayor of Baltimore. Congressman D'Alesandro advised Agent Bartlett that since he had been on the Appropriations Committee, he has been back of the Director and the Bureau one hundred percent, and further, that he was vitally interested in and completely satisfied with the results of the Bureau's work.

Hoover sent warm congratulations to D'Alesandro upon his November 1946 re-election to the House and then his May 1947 election as Baltimore Mayor, and after leaving Congress for City Hall D'Alesandro wrote Hoover by letter dated May 14, 1947:

Thank you very much for message congratulating me on my election as Mayor of the City of Baltimore. I was most pleased to receive your good wishes and assure you that I will do my utmost to give the people of

*Baltimore an efficient and outstanding
administration. I, too, will miss you and
many other friends in Washington but I am
grateful for the proximity of our two cities
which will afford the opportunity for frequent
visits when and if time permits. Whenever
you are in Baltimore, please make it a point
to visit me at City Hall.*

(Kennedy, Hoover, Kennedy)

*Meanwhile, the allegations against
D'Alesandro continued to pile up. Finally, in
January 1961 President John F. Kennedy
requested the G-men to address allegations of*

D'Alesandro's involvement with Baltimore hoodlums; with favoritism in awarding city contracts and protection for political contributors and the prosecution of local cases. President Kennedy wanted to appoint D'Alesandro to the United States Renegotiation Board which was a government watchdog against profit gouging by defense contractors. A February 6, 1961 memo from Hoover to the Baltimore and Washington Field Offices cautiously advises: "The White House has requested that we proceed with a special inquiry investigation but that if substantial derogatory information were developed, we should report this and discontinue any further inquiries because substantiation of any of the allegations would eliminate D'Alesandro."

The FBI inquiry was a perfunctory exercise with little digging which vainly attempted to address two decades of allegations in less than two months, and of course some witnesses had lost their memories and others had died or otherwise disappeared.

For example, Peter Galiano, the convicted boxer involved with Magliano's draft-dodging scheme who told Special Agent James V. Sullivan in January 1947 that D'Alesandro was a constant companion of both Magliano and Cataneo, more than a decade later when pressed by the FBI said on February 8, 1961 his statement was only rumor and hearsay, and he could not recall who gave him this information or whether or not there was any truth to these allegations. However, there was independent corroboration for at least some of Galiano's earlier allegations. The FBI notes that during the investigation of the Selective Service fraud case SA James V. Sullivan had occasion to be at the American Ship Cleaning Company Offices in Baltimore on several occasions and had seen appointee D'Alesandro in the company of John Cataneo. Moreover, Special Agent Sullivan in 1947 had received from another informant similar information concerning D'Alesandro's ties to Cataneo and Magliano, and this informant further advised that Cataneo also supposedly was well-regarded by D'Alesandro because he had control of a large Italian vote in Baltimore.

D'Alesandro also was accused by highly-credible police officers of providing protection to Baltimore hoodlums. For example, in 1945, Captain John R. Rollman, Western District, Baltimore Police

Department, Baltimore, Maryland, furnished information to the Baltimore Office of the Federal Bureau of Investigation concerning one Charles F. Cammarata. According to Captain Rollman, Cammarata had gotten away with all sorts of criminal activities in the Western District due to the protection of Maryland United States Representative Thomas D'Alesandro, and Cammarata was alleged to be gambling in various crap and card games in Baltimore. Once again, the FBI never did anything about these allegations at the time they were made, and in 1961 when the G-men finally got around to looking into them Captain Rollman since had died and Cammarata's current whereabouts are unknown. A March 15, 1961 FBI memo reports that Cammarata may have been last seen in Havana, Cuba in the mid-1950s where he allegedly had some connection with Clark's Tropicana Night Club, and may now be residing in Miami, FL where he reportedly owned apartment houses; however, perhaps content to let sleeping dogs lie, the FBI never followed up on these tips in an attempt to reach Cammarata about the alleged protection he received from D'Alesandro while operating in Baltimore in the 1940s.

Another serious allegation against D'Alesandro was that he had received kickbacks from building developer Dominic Piracci on city contracts. Piracci's account ledger included several payments totaling $11,000 to D'Alesandro which he later erased to keep the information from investigators. The developer later explained that the payments were legitimate loans to Mrs. D'Alesandro to finance her cosmetics business which since had been fully repaid, and he doctored the documents only to save the D'Alesandro family from embarrassment and from further trouble given a criminal investigation into his business practices. In April 1954 Piracci was found guilty of conspiracy to defraud the city of $42,996 in connection with the construction of an off-street parking garage in Baltimore, and also found guilty for obstruction of justice in that he submitted to a Baltimore City Grand Jury a completely phony ledger to conceal $35,000 in weekly payments to the Peoples Holding Corporation whose officers were also charged with conspiracy to defraud Baltimore City in an off-street parking garage contract. Mrs. D'Alesandro testified on Piracci's behalf at his criminal trial, and although she insisted the loans from Piracci *were repaid there was no documentary evidence to corroborate that testimony. The supposed repayments were made in cash rather than by check. Mrs. D'Alesandro's testimony may have saved her husband from criminal liability but could not save his then-bid to become Maryland's governor. The D'Alesandro's son Thomas III later married Piracci's daughter Margaret.*

The Piracci trial at which Mrs. D'Alesandro testified immediately was followed by a child gang rape trial against the Mayor's 20-year old son Franklin Roosevelt D'Alesandro. The FBI describes the ugly case in a January 30, 1961 memo as follows:

During the summer of 1953, Mayor D'Alesandro's son, Franklin Roosevelt D'Alesandro, aged twenty, was one of fourteen youths charged with having committed rape or perverted practices on two girls, aged eleven and thirteen, during July of that year. It was reported that Franklin Roosevelt D'Alesandro was the only one of twelve of those tried at that time who was successful in obtaining an acquittal. Following this acquittal, a Baltimore, Maryland, Grand Jury indicted Franklin Roosevelt D'Alesandro on charges of having committed perjury in that he had lied during the afore-mentioned trial on charges of rape. In addition, James H. Pollack, Baltimore City political boss, was reportedly also indicted on the charge of obstruction of justice in that he had attempted to influence testimony of several of the youthful defendants who had been tried with Franklin Roosevelt D'Alesandro. It was reported that Franklin Roosevelt D'Alesandro was tried on the above charge of perjury at Salisbury, Maryland, during 1954, following a change of venue, and was found not guilty.

A Feb 27, 1961 FBI memo states that according to one informant, the consensus of opinion among persons connected with law enforcement that appointee's, D'Alesandro's, son acquitted of rape because of brilliant fashion defense attorney handled the case. Franklin Roosevelt D'Alesandro was represented by Joseph Sherbow who managed to sever his client from the other defendants and ensured his trial went first so any convictions against the others would not prejudice him. Apparently, D'Alesandro believed that his son was guilty of the charge, and prior to trial urged him to plead guilty and take his medicine.

The corruption charges and his son's rape trial all had become more than Mayor D'Alesandro could bear, and he suffered a nervous breakdown. D'Alesandro was admitted to the Bon Secours Hospital in Maryland where he rested from March 10 through July 12, 1954. During this period according to an FBI memo, the Baltimore City Police Department had two men assigned to protect the appointee, D'Alesandro, and also had two men guarding his home at 245 Albemarle Street for unknown reasons and a local paper carried a picture of him in his hospital room seated in front of a television set, dressed in a dressing gown.

Most of the FBI's special inquiry into D'Alesandro involved brief interviews with his political cronies, personal friends and family members who insisted the Mayor was a swell guy. The allegations against D'Alesandro involving public graft and hoodlum associations were conveniently ignored or gratuitously explained away, and on March 28, 1961 he was sworn in as a member of the United States Renegotiation Board by President Kennedy. D'Alesandro's

(D'Alesandro Family)

Nancy Pelosi's father and brother Franklin were not the only family members to be involved in corruption. Nancy Pelosi and her husband Paul Pelosi have also engaged in corrupt activities that earned them and close acquaintances money. Often using political influence to ensure projects moved forward or seizing opportunities based upon information not available to others are tools used by the powerful to became wealthy. The Treasure Island Development project is a good example.

Treasure island is an island and former military base in San Francisco Bay. When military bases close they usually leave a financial burden to the city due to loss of jobs belonging to civilians who support the operations of the base. Their sale usually requires that priority be given to buyers providing programs including affordable housing and businesses to stimulate job creation. Priority is often given to building housing and a community for homeless veterans.

(Treasure Island)

Treasure Island is a little different. It is a highly valuable property near the wealth of the Bay Area, San Francisco, and Silicon Valley. The proximity to the city, serenity of the bay and incredible views makes this property a gold mine for high-end developers. Pelosi worked with local officials to ensure this property would not be wasted on projects for the poor. She also helped ensure that members of her family would benefit from the project.

According to Malkin, Michelle, 2010, Payments to the Navy could rise to $105 million, funded by private companies and revenue from developing the former Navy base into a model 21st century neighborhood.

Pelosi has used her power to push the crony-infested project for years. She pushed aggressively for legislative language that would have forced the military to fork over high-value property at no cost to local communities. And as the Washington Times recounted last fall, she presided over a "den of corruption" to secure the coveted property:

Treasure Island is not a case of a small town that has relied on a local military base for its livelihood for decades. It is a land grab by politicians for well-connected developers. Tony Hall, the former executive director of the Treasure Island Development Authority, told us the city's effort to develop the island is a "den of corruption." Treasure Island Community Development, the prospective developer for Treasure Island, was granted a no-bid contract by the city.

At the core of Treasure Island Community Development are high-powered California Democratic lobbyist Darius Anderson and supermarket magnate Ronald W. Burkle. Both are well-known financial backers of San Francisco's Democratic Mayor Gavin Newsom.

A proposed Treasure Island development plan slates 90 percent of the developed acreage for residential use, 7 percent for commercial property and 3 percent for parking. An illustration shows about a dozen high-rise blocks of shoreline condominiums with stunning views of the city, plus 300 acres of park and recreation land. This would hardly be "affordable housing," given the $5 billion investment that Mrs. Pelosi claims would have to be recouped by the developer. The only long-term jobs created from this plan would be for maids and doormen for the high rollers privileged enough to live there.

The Navy merits praise for holding the line in defense of a market-based transfer of Treasure Island. Cloaking this land grab under a measure to help local communities suffering the disruption of military base closure is disgraceful.

Fog City Journal shines more light on the Pelosi cronyism behind the deal:

Likewise, the person who appoints the people on TIDA and similar boards is also a key player, for he or she must be guided to select members who can be trusted to vote favorably to one's interests. That's the entitlement portion of the Big Three: garnering approvals that entitle one to development and maximize profits by up-zoning the land. (Up-zoning means changing the rules to allow more profitable development than would otherwise be allowed.).

That's why forming relationships between would-be developers and appointing officials is crucial. Lobbyists like Platinum's Darius Anderson and Jay Wallace specialize in building those relationships, sometimes by finding sources of cash reserves for campaign contributions, or occasionally hosting key fundraisers. Wallace was at one-time Pelosi's campaign manager.

When Anderson held a fundraiser a couple of years ago to retire Mayor Newsom's campaign debt, it raised eyebrows, but it is what lobbyists do. They specialize in creating access for themselves and for clients with the people who make appointments, sign or promote legislation, and grant entitlements to develop, all of which have big profit implications.

It's easy to conclude that clients are getting their money's worth from Platinum and friends, especially when the client is Platinum itself. TIDA has granted to Platinum the uncontested contract to be the sole developer of Treasure Island, with the master plan component going to Anderson's other company, Kenwood Investments.

Platinum's development entity has been handed the Treasure Island bounty. Given the Pelosi and Newsom history of enthusiasm for developing the Presidio, we should hope it's not too late to keep a close watch and short leash on Treasure Island developments. Unfortunately, this means paying attention to the entire family. That would include even the new president on the Commission on the Environment, Paul Pelosi, Jr., who is Nancy Pelosi's son and Gavin Newsom's cousin. As for TIDA itself, the mayor appointed all the members; all but one is a City Hall official.

Who else will benefit from the arrangement? Certainly, Lennar Corporation will. They are a partner with Platinum's Treasure Island Community Developers. Lennar has experience developing former military bases, and is one of the country's largest residential housing builders.

By what could solicitously be called a coincidence, Laurence Pelosi was president of acquisitions for Lennar. He is Nancy Pelosi's nephew, and currently works as executive director of Morgan Stanley's real estate division.

Congress does not follow the same set of rules that ordinary citizens must follow. They voted themselves an exception to the illegality of insider trading. This is bizarre given that they are the ones in a position to influence stock prices because they certainly have knowledge of upcoming events that could influence stock values not available to the ordinary investor. While it is not illegal for congress to engage in insider trading, it is still considered to be highly unethical. Nancy and Paul Pelosi have made considerable money through insider trading.

According to Newsmax, 2011, Former House Speaker Nancy Pelosi bought stock in initial public offerings (IPOs) that earned hefty returns while she had access to insider information that would have been illegal for an average citizen to trade with even though it's perfectly legal for elected officials.

(U.S. Capital)

In the case of elected officials, this secret information ranges from timely details on lucrative federal contracts to legislation that can cause companies' stocks to rise and fall dramatically. Lawmakers have exempted themselves from the laws that govern every other citizen. Regulations carry hefty prison sentences and fines for any other citizen who trades stocks with private information on companies that can affect their stock price.

Pelosi and her husband have participated in at least eight IPOs while having access to information directly relating to the companies involved. One of those came in 2008, from Visa, just as a troublesome piece of legislation that would have hurt credit card companies, began making its way through the House.

Undisturbed by a potential conflict of interest the Pelosi's purchased 5,000 shares of Visa at the initial price of $44 dollars. Two days later it was trading at $64. The credit card legislation never made it to the floor of the House.

There are all sorts of forms of honest grafts that congressmen engage in that allow them to become very, very wealthy, not the least of which is Insider trading on the stock market. If you are a member of Congress, insider trading laws are deemed not to apply. If you sit on a healthcare committee and you know that Medicare, for example, is considering not reimbursing for a certain drug that's market moving information. Members can trade stock using that information and do so legally, creating a great profit-making opportunity.

Nancy Pelosi is an outspoken advocate for open borders and sanctuary cities, which theoretically protect illegal aliens. Given her public position, it seemed ironic that a speech she was to give about amnesty for Deferred Action for Childhood Arrivals (DACA) was interrupted and hijacked by a group calling her a liar and calling for amnesty for all illegal aliens. The people on that stage knew the truth, as did Pelosi.

There are reasons she advocates for open borders and sanctuary cities to protect undocumented workers. She and many of her wealthy cronies rely on these workers. She uses exclusively non-union, illegal workers on her Napa Vineyard.

Without a steady stream of illegal workers to exploit, she would not be able to make a profit off her high-end wines.

It is widely accepted by both sides of the aisle that most illegal immigrants are here for economic reasons, or to escape violent crime in their own countries. Once here they do not enjoy the protections granted by U.S. labor laws. They are unlikely to report crimes against them to police. They are at high risk of being exploited by employers and others.

Democrats are bringing in slave labor for themselves and their rich friends. Hollywood types will have cheap baby sitters, gardeners, maids, and vulnerable women looking for jobs for their sponsors to sexually harass and exploit.

Democrats always pretend that they're bringing in illegal immigrants because they care about people. If they cared about people, they would start by caring about the plight of fellow citizens who are living in poverty.

Democrats are exploiting poverty both in this country and outside this country, for their own selfish benefits when they lie to their followers that they like illegal immigrants. Illegal immigrants have no way to work legally in the United States which means they can only work for slave wages for masters who will keep them silent with threats of deportation.

Part of the fortune of Nancy Pelosi, defender of the working man, is a Napa Valley vineyard worth $25 million that she owns with her husband. The vineyard produces expensive grapes for high-end wines. Napa grapes bring up to $4,000 a ton compared with $300 a ton for, say, San Joaquin grapes.

But Pelosi, winner of the 2003 Cesar Chavez award from the United Farm Workers, hires only nonunion workers and sells these grapes to nonunion wineries.

Pelosi's steadfast opposition to any attempts to enhance border security and stem the flow of illegal immigration into the U.S. becomes all the more interesting since she is among rich employers who financially benefit from cheap foreign labor.

Pelosi has not been a fan of employer sanctions against the hiring of illegal aliens. In 2003, she accused immigration officers of conducting raids on Wal-Mart stores that led to the arrest of more than 300 illegal aliens.

Half of the migrant labor force in the Napa Valley consisted of undocumented workers, without whom not one bottle of wine would get made there.

While most illegal immigrants are here to better their lives, others are criminals escaping their country and taking advantage of the poorly enforced immigration laws. Law enforcement is hindered by so-called sanctuary cities which refuse to turn illegal immigrants accused of crimes over to the federal enforcement agencies.

Pelosi abuses lowest paid workers to increase her stock profits. Nancy Pelosi's home district includes San Francisco. Star-Kist Tuna's headquarters are in San Francisco, Pelosi's home district. Star-Kist is owned by Del Monte Foods which is a major contributor to Nancy Pelosi. Star-

Kist is the major employer in American Samoa employing 75% of the Samoan work force. Paul Pelosi, Nancy's husband, owns $17 million dollars of Star-Kist stock.

In January 2007 when the minimum wage was increased from $5.15 to $7.25, Pelosi had American Samoa exempted from the increase, so Del Monte would not have to pay the higher wage. This would make Del Monte products less expensive than their competition's.

When a huge bailout bill was passed, Pelosi added an earmark to the final bill adding $33 million dollars for an economic development credit in American Samoa.

According to Markay, Lachlan, 2014, *The top Democrat in the House of Representatives steered more than a billion dollars in subsidies to a light rail project that benefitted a company run by a high-dollar Democratic donor and in which her husband is a major investor.*

When cloud computing giant Salesforce sold a large plot of land to the Golden State Warriors in April, it had House Minority Leader Nancy Pelosi to thank for helping to swell real estate prices in the area.

Pelosi has worked for more than a decade to steer taxpayer funds to a light rail project in San Francisco's Mission Bay neighborhood, where Salesforce had planned a new campus. Experts say the project boosted the value of Mission Bay real estate.

The company's CEO, Marc Benioff, is a high-dollar Democratic donor. Pelosi and her leadership PAC are among the recipients of his generous campaign contributions. Pelosi's husband is also a major Salesforce investor.

(Salesforce Building, San Francisco)

Nancy Pelosi
In Her Own Words

"The Confederate statues in the halls of Congress have always been reprehensible, if Republicans are serious about rejecting white supremacy, I call upon Speaker Ryan to join Democrats to remove the Confederate statues from the Capitol immediately." (Nancy Pelosi)

It is strange that after 30 years in congress, Ms. Pelosi suddenly takes offense to these statues. She challenges Speaker of the House Ryan to remove the statues. She seems to forget that she was Speaker of the House for four years prior to Ryan. She never took any action to remove the statues she claimed offended her so much.

Removing statues does not change history, which seems to be the true goal of the Democratic Party. The Democratic Party was founded on opposition to Abraham Lincoln and opposition to the abolition of slavery. Democrats built the confederacy. Democrats also founded the Ku Klux Klan to fight Republicans.

Robert E. Lee had a long military history aside from the Civil War. He was offered to command the Union Army. Lee had no attachment to the south, but he did to his home state of Virginia and as such joined the south. Ironically, at the start of the Civil War, Robert E. Lee owned no slaves, but Ulysses S. Grant owned one, (his family owned more). After the Civil War, Lee was an important force in reuniting the north and the south.

Pelosi's demands that confederate statues be torn down shows she has a lack of knowledge of history, including the history of her own party. The hypocrisy becomes ever apparent when one considered her father, Thomas D'Alesandro dedicated confederate statues in Baltimore.

(Lee and Jackson Statue, Baltimore)

"Every month that we do not have an economic recovery package 500 million Americans lose their jobs." (Nancy Pelosi)

Of course, this statement is flawed. Our country only had 307 million people and there are only 136 million jobs.

Congress must be insulated from reality. An economic recovery package is used to make small corrections in failed policies which had adverse effects on the populace. It should not be a staple of American life; good policies should be.

Small businesses count for the bulk of jobs and new job creation. Obamacare placed an unfair burden on these businesses and their workers. Rather than pay the outrageous fees for Obamacare, many small businesses were forced to either cut all workers to part time status or fire them completely. Unless the recovery package has a no Obamacare clause for small businesses, there will be little change.

No actions taken by the government should ever put 500 million, or 136 million jobs at risk. Government should never be that powerful.

"I believe in natural gas as a clean, cheap alternative to fossil fuels. It's cheap, abundant and clean compared to fossil fuels." (**Nancy Pelosi**)

Nancy Pelosi gets half credit for this comment. Natural gas is an awesome fuel. It burns cleanly with no harmful waste. If not burned and left in its natural state it has a much more significant impact on the level of greenhouse gases than carbon dioxide. It is definitely superior to other fossil fuels.

Where she failed, well, natural gas is a fossil fuel.

Even if we stopped using vehicles that run on oil products, we would still need oil.

(Natural Gas Plant)

Nancy Pelosi likely knew just the most basic information about natural gas. Her motivation was not protecting the environment so much as it was an effort to increase her own wealth by pushing legislation supporting natural gas industries.

in November 2007, Pelosi bought $500,000 in the IPO for Quest Energy Partners before proceeding to champion the natural gas-related legislation that stood to significantly benefit the company. When Tom Brokaw asked her whether her significant personal investments in natural gas represented a conflict of interest, Pelosi shrugged off the question by hiding behind the crony capitalist's false credo: "That's the marketplace."

(Natural Gas Storage Tanks)

"We have an estimated 12 million illegal immigrants in our country who need our help along with millions of unemployed minorities. Stock market profits taxes could go a long way to guarantee these people the standard of living they would like to have as "Americans." **(Nancy Pelosi)**

There are a few assumptions democrats always make. The first is that illegal immigrants are U.S. citizens deserving of resources derived by taxing Americans. Legal is legal; Illegal is not.

Nancy Pelosi should be aware of this because she only hires illegals for her vineyard because she can pay them less than is required for American citizens and she does not need to afford them protections of U.S. labor laws. If she cares about the plight of illegal aliens she could start by affording them protections under U.S. labor law and she can pay her workers minimum wage.

The second is that minorities are dependent on the help of government. Minorities need a level playing field, but aside from that are capable of success.

Third are that minorities vote democrat. Minorities do not vote as one big group and have varied political opinions.

Fourth, there are substantially more white Americans living in poverty than any other racial demographic.

Stock market profit tax is also known as Capital gains tax. It is a real thing already and does not need to be reinvented. A percentage of whatever money is gained through stocks is meant to be paid when the stock is sold. Selling stock, however lowers the overall value of the stock.

Most people who own stock, like Nancy Pelosi, are aware of loopholes that counteract capital gains tax payment. Capital gains tax is not earmarked for any special programs, including those for the poor.

(New York Stock Exchange)

"First Bush cut taxes for the rich and the economy has rebounded with new record low unemployment rates, which only means wealthy employers are getting even wealthier at the expense of the underpaid working class." (**Nancy Pelosi**)

The rich and the poor have a symbiotic relationship. Neither can make money without the other. If President Bush cut taxes for the rich and the economy rebounded, it would benefit both rich and poor.

If unemployment rates are at a record low, that means that people who were not being paid, are now employed. These people benefit by having a paycheck. The wealthy get wealthier which allows for more jobs to be created in the future, benefiting the unemployed.

As for the underpaid working class, there is no impact one way or the other. Pelosi may cry foul when the rich are given tax breaks, but she is secretly thrilled because she and her husband are very wealthy with a joint net worth of approximately 250 million dollars.

"We haven't really gotten the credit for what we have done." (Nancy Pelosi)

According to Seidl, John, 2010, Pelosi suggested that voter discontent is simply due to misinformation. We haven't really gotten the credit for what we have done, but we will take it to the voters and have a Democratic majority to follow through on it.

She also takes criticism as a sign of success: "If I were not effective, they wouldn't care about me, but they must stop me because we have made this important change. She quipped, "it helps me raise money."

But the irony may be that the reason Americans are upset with Democrats, and why so many are predicting wide Republican victories is exactly because constituents recognize what Dems have accomplished: mainly controversial financial reform and soaring deficits accompanied by a widely unpopular health care bill. Pelosi promised "no new deficit spending" when she became Speaker in 2007, the national debt increased by $5 trillion. Pelosi, the 60th speaker of the U.S. House of Representatives, has added more to the national debt than the first 57 House speakers combined.

Pelosi suggests that voters don't really understand what Democrats did for them, and are the victims of a misinformation campaign.

Voters were quite aware of what Pelosi and the democrats had done. They just did not agree with it and in 2016, not only did they reject the Democratic Presidential candidate, but also voted democrats out of the house and senate.

(Pelosi, looking confused)

***"We are not going back to the failed policies of the past. We are fighting for the middle class!"**
(Nancy Pelosi)*

According to Rucker, Phillip, 2010, *Nancy Pelosi, the most powerful woman in American politics, lost her job as speaker of the House on as voters delivered a sharp rebuke to the party she helped lead.*

Her steely manner and the progressive policies she championed made her a favorite target for resurgent Republicans nationwide. Pelosi's face appeared in more GOP attack ads than any other Democrat, including President Obama.

Pelosi had seized upon a rare Democratic alignment across government to orchestrate deals that she saw as historic and remarkable, but which seemed intrusive and ideological to a broadening swath of the U.S. electorate. In the end, it cost her the powerful gavel.

In the end, Pelosi was a speaker who couldn't speak up for herself. In the final run-up to a midterm election that she knew could be a dramatic rebuke, Pelosi rarely campaigned in public. She shuttled between private fundraisers and then hunkered down with

Pelosi's pledge that she was fighting for the middle class, did not ring true. Given that she has been in office for 30 years, what damage did the failed policies of the past cause that she must declare a break from the past and a new declaration that congress is now there to fight for the middle class.

(Pelosi and Ryan)

"Think of an economy where people could be an artist or a photographer or a writer without worrying about keeping their day job in order to have health insurance." (Nancy Pelosi)

Politicians seem to think that the highest priority for voters is that they have access to health care. People work "day jobs" to pay their rent and feed their family. Until the government became involved, Health Care was a benefit. Once the government became involved and rates skyrocketed, it became a financial burden for many, as the money allotted for rent and feeding the family was involuntarily moved to cover mandatory health care.

Small businesses were also hit hard. The burden posed by health care payments caused workers to be forced into part time work, fired or the business simply closed.

Ms. Pelosi may not realize that being an artist, writer or photographer often is a person's only job. It is not a hobby. Sadly, the burden of mandatory health care hits these independent workers hardest and may even be the impetus for them having to get a second job.

*"**The impact of climate change is a tremendous risk to the security and well-being of our countries.**" (Nancy Pelosi)*

The precursor to climate change was global warming. After empirical evidence suggested the world was getting cooler not warmer, the democrats and their media minions began referring to the theory as climate change. If we accept climate change is occurring, the next question would be whether the change is natural or man-made.

According to Adams, Mike, 2014, NASA and the NOAA have been caught red-handed altering historical temperature data to produce a "climate change narrative" that defies reality. This finding, originally documented on the Real Science website, is detailed here.

We now know that historical temperature data for the continental United States were deliberately altered by NASA and NOAA scientists in a politically-motivated attempt to rewrite history and claim global warming is causing U.S. temperatures to trend upward. The data actually shows that we are in a cooling trend, not a warming trend.

According to Hayward, John, 2015, *As climate data continues its stubborn refusal to conform to doomsday models, global-warming activists have focused much of their effort on attempting to discredit critics, apparently in the belief that "science" means suppressing inconvenient information to make hypotheses look better.*

A major theme running through these efforts is the supposed financial "conflicts of interest" facing scientists whose work is not funded by ideologically pure supporters of catastrophic man-made climate change theories. To put it bluntly, the warmists insist that anyone who disagrees with them is a dishonest puppet of reckless and greedy fossil fuel companies.

It is not known how Pelosi equates climate change with a countries security. Perhaps she believes that if the world heats up, people will migrate towards the poles, of if the world becomes colder people might migrate to the equator.

Given that in 100 years, the maximum estimate of temperature change is just above 1 degree and global temperatures vary over 100 degrees from equator to poles, the earth will be fine for some time to come.

There was still a great deal of money for investors to claim based upon the governments push towards a climate change agenda. Al Gore, the poster child for global warming became the first "Green" billionaire based upon his investment in companies that would benefit from the climate change hysteria.

Nancy Pelosi and her Husband, Paul Pelosi, also made significant money off fore-knowledge of government involvement with certain green companies.

According to Markay, Lachlan, 2016, House Democratic Leader Nancy Pelosi's husband bought up to quarter million dollars of stock in a now financially troubled green energy company just weeks before it announced a major 2014 acquisition that sent stock prices soaring, public records show.

SunEdison told regulators last week that it is eyeing bankruptcy under the weight of $11.7 million in debt. But in late 2014, investors were bullish on the company, which manufactures and operates solar and wind power facilities.

Its 2014 purchase of wind energy company First Wind "further bolstered the reputation of the company," wrote one market-watcher at the time. "Perhaps unsurprisingly, SunEdison's stock soared an astounding 29% on news of this acquisition alone."

Pelosi's husband, Paul Pelosi, had invested just in time. He bought between $100,000 and $250,000 in SunEdison stock on Oct. 24, 2014, according to congressional financial disclosures. The company announced its First Wind acquisition on Nov. 17.

(The Once Lucrative SunEdison company)

"But we have to pass the bill so you can find out what is in it, away from the fog of the controversy." (Nancy Pelosi)

Nancy Pelosi was one of the most outspoken supporters of Obamacare. The major controversy about this legislation was that it was very large, and it appeared to be being pushed quickly through congress. It did not appear that members would have time to read the entire act and adequately debate the pros and cons.

Seeking national attention by being the democrat's cheerleader for Obamacare, she was the most likely focal point of media attention. As she spoke globally and was unable to answer anything specific; It became apparent to most that she had not read the Act, nor did she know any useful details about it. This lead to her most famous quote about the need to pass a bill before we can find out what is in it. This action would be tantamount to a teacher grading a paper before it was written; a judge making a sentence before a case has been heard; or a credit card company charging you for things they anticipate you will purchase.

Pelosi would claim that it was her passionate desire for everyone to have affordable health care that drove her enthusiasm. For many workers and small businesses, Obamacare was a nightmare. Pelosi passed it, the American people found out what was in it.

As with most things she advocates for in congress, Pelosi had a financial interest in passing Obamacare.

> According to Lucas, Fred, 2008, *House Speaker Nancy Pelosi dismissed any notion that her sponsorship of Medicaid legislation that would likely help her husband's financial holdings in a pharmaceutical company presented a conflict of interest.*

> *She also stressed there was no need to divest any stock that her husband holds in Johnson & Johnson, a company that makes and markets HIV-related drugs that could be helped by the Early Treatment of HIV Act, which Pelosi introduced last summer. "Absolutely not," Pelosi said when asked if she would consider divesting.*

> *Pelosi's husband owns between $250,000 and $500,000 stock in Johnson & Johnson, the company that markets the anemia drug Procrit used by HIV patients and others with anemia. Procrit is manufactured by Amgen, a pharmaceutical firm based in Thousand Oaks, Calif.*

On July 27, 2007, 28 Amgen executives contributed more than $20,000 to Pelosi's re-election campaign. See Previous Story

On July 30, the Center for Medicare and Medicaid Services announced it would tighten the rules on paying for anemia drugs such as Procrit.

On Aug. 2, Pelosi introduced the HIV bill that would give states the option to allow patients who are HIV-positive, but do not have AIDS, to qualify for Medicaid coverage earlier in the course of the virus. Currently, Medicaid coverage doesn't kick in until a patient develops AIDS.

Most state Medicaid systems, including those in California, New York, and New Jersey, cover Procrit now. The Early Treatment of HIV Act, if passed, would expand the number of people eligible for Medicaid coverage for the drug.

In addition to the 28 separate contributions Pelosi received last July from Amgen employees, seven other contributions were made by executives in the months of July and August, for a total of $30,050 to Pelosi's re-election campaign. Also, Amgen's political action committee gave Pelosi's campaign a *total of $10,000 last year. Employees of the company had not previously contributed such large amounts to Pelosi's campaign, according to the Center for Responsive Politics, which tracks campaign contributions going back to 1992.*

This has prompted some public interest groups to allege a conflict of interest given Pelosi's potential financial benefit from the legislation.

(Amgen, Thousand Oaks, CA.)

"We're sad about some of the losses of members of great seniority and distinction in the Congress, and some very new members, who will no longer be serving with us." (Nancy Pelosi)

According to Sanchez, Ray, 2010, *House Speaker Nancy Pelosi said today she has "no regrets" one day after a Republican landslide stripped her of the power that defined her historic tenure as the first female speaker of the House.*

"We believe we did the right thing, and we worked very hard in our campaigns to convey that to the American people," she said. "Nine and a half percent unemployment is a very eclipsing event. If people don't have a job, they're not too interested in how you intend for them to have a job. They want to see results."

More than any other Democrat other than President Obama, Pelosi became the face of GOP attack ads. Michael Steele, the Republican National Committee chairman, campaigned around the country in a bus plastered with the slogan, "Fire Pelosi." "They have used me as a personification of health care and the rest, I take that as a compliment."

She conceded she was surprised by the magnitude of the Democratic loss and thought that as many as 20 close elections were going to go Democratic.

"Given that there are now 60-plus defeated Democrat House members urgently seeking jobs due to Nancy Pelosi's failed leadership, we welcome her decision to run for House Minority Leader based on her proven ability to create jobs for Republican lawmakers," Ken Spain, communications director at the National Republican Congressional Committee, said. "The definition of insanity is doing the same thing over and over again, and expecting a different result. Of course, if House Democrats are willing to sacrifice more of their members in 2012 for the glory of Nancy Pelosi, we are happy to oblige them."

In 2010 Democrats were being rebuked by the voters. The loss was a direct reflection of people's dissatisfaction with the performance of Pelosi and Obama. Both remained oblivious. Pelosi did lose many long-term allies at once. She expressed her sadness to see them go.

The marble ceiling Mrs. Pelosi is speaking of is usually referred to as a glass ceiling. It is an imaginary barrier demarcating women's level of success. Once a woman rises to a new level, it is said that she has broken through the glass ceiling, thus opening the barrier for future women to rise as well.

Trying to break through glass with your head may be difficult but it can be done without significant injury. Trying to break a marble ceiling with your head is sure to cause brain damage. Pelosi apparently broke through a marble ceiling.

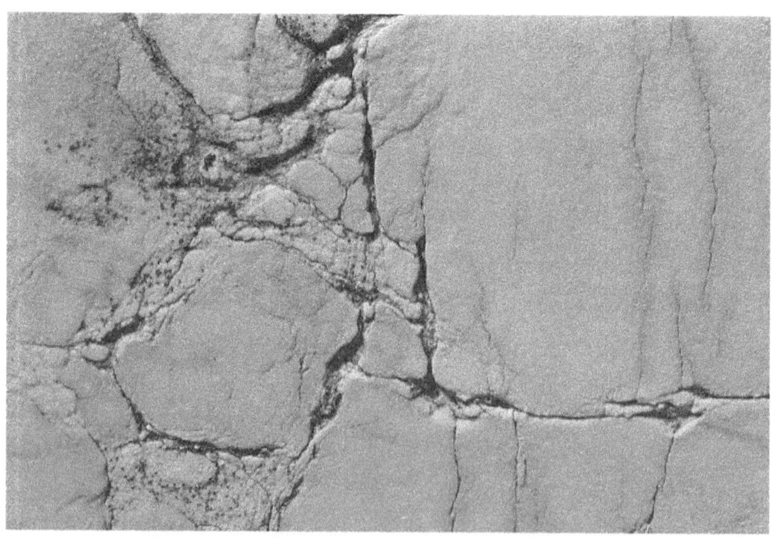

(Marble is much tougher than glass)

"I have deep emotions about the American people. If I were to cry for anything, I would cry for them and the policies that they're about to face." (Nancy Pelosi)

Mrs. Pelosi made this comment after the landslide democrat loss in the house and senate in 2010. Her main concern was that the Republican controlled house would remove Obamacare.

Nancy Pelosi never realized that the majority of the public did not support Obamacare. They did not support the lies that participants could keep their doctors. They did not like the lies that cost would go down when for most they went up. They did not like the limited options for insurance coverage.

Voting against democrats in 2010 was strongly driven by those who wanted Obamacare repealed. They felt it was illegal for the government to tell you that you must pay a private company for care.

It appears that members in congress on both sides of the aisle may have put too much faith in the trustworthiness of the insurance companies. It may be that they deferred to the expertise of these companies and thus did not do proper research on their own. It may be that the act was too complex for many in congress to understand. Whether

Obamacare needs fixing or replacing is a current debate.

According to Potter, Wendell, 2015, *When members of Congress caved to demands from the insurance industry and ditched their plan to establish a "public option" health plan, the lawmakers also ditched one of their favorite talking points, that a government-run plan was necessary to "keep insurers honest."*

Getting rid of a government-run insurance option was the industry's top objective during the health care reform debate. Private insurers set out to persuade President Obama and Congressional leaders that they were trustworthy. Lawmakers were led to believe, for one thing, that insurers could be trusted to offer policies that would continue to give Americans' access to the doctors they had developed relationships with and wanted to keep. And they were persuaded that insurers wouldn't think of engaging in bait-and-switch tactics that would leave folks with less coverage than they thought they were buying.

Obama insisted on a public option for months after he was elected. He said on July 18, 2009, "Any plan I sign must include an insurance exchange—a one-stop-shopping marketplace where you can compare the benefits, costs and track records of a variety of plans, including a public option to increase competition and keep insurance companies honest..."

Soon after that, though, he began to waffle. It became clear to me as well as public option supporters in Congress that industry lobbyists had gotten to him.

If Congress failed to create a public option to compete with private insurers, "the bill it sends to the President might as well have been called "The Insurance Industry Profit Protection and Enhancement Act."

Insurers had spent years investing in Sen. Joe Lieberman, a former Democrat-turned-Independent. Insurers had contributed nearly half a million dollars to his campaigns over the years.

The Democrats needed Lieberman's vote to get reform passed, and insurers knew it. Lieberman said he would vote for the bill only if the public option was stripped out. Lieberman accused public option supporters of having an ulterior motive. "A public option plan is unnecessary," he told Fox News. "It has been put forward, I'm convinced, by people who really want the government to take over all of health insurance."

Millions of Americans who have signed up for coverage on the Obamacare exchanges are finding out that they will not get any coverage if they continue going to the doctors they've been going to for years.

On the other side of the country, California Insurance Commissioner Dave Jones last month issued an emergency regulation after getting a flood of calls from folks who said health insurers had swindled them.

"Californians and California businesses deserve better than what they have gotten from most health insurers and HMOs," Jones said at the time. "Health insurers' medical provider directories have been inaccurate, misleading consumers into signing up with a health insurer for access to a doctor, specialist, or hospital only to learn that these medical providers are not actually a part of the health insurer's network."

"Bipartisanship is nice, but it cannot be a substitute for action, not having it cannot prevent us from going forward." (Nancy Pelosi)

Bipartisanship is the key to moving forward, it is not simply, nice. If one party has a majority, they can potentially pass any votes that require a simple majority but being a member of a party does not necessarily mean everyone within that party agrees on every issue.

If a vote requires a super-majority then it is essential for bipartisan agreement. It is not a substitute for action, it is the only way action can occur.

"Social Security has never failed to pay promised benefits, and Democrats will fight to make sure that Republicans do not turn a guaranteed benefit into a guaranteed gamble." (Nancy Pelosi)

Desilver, Drew, 2015, *For much of its history, Social Security was a strictly pay-as-you-go system, with current tax receipts funding current benefits. That changed in 1983, when Congress raised the payroll taxes that provide the bulk of Social Security's revenue, to build up a cushion for the coming onslaught of Baby Boomer retirees. For nearly three decades, the system took in far more revenue than it paid out in benefits; the surplus was invested in special non-tradeable Treasury bonds, with interest credited to the system's two trust funds As of July 31, those trust funds together held $2.83 trillion in Treasuries. Some people characterize that as the government "borrowing from" or "raiding" Social Security.*

But since 2010, Social Security's cash expenses have exceeded its cash receipts. Negative cash flow last year was about $74 billion, according to the latest trustees' report, and this year the gap is projected to be around $84 billion. While the

Borrowing from the Social Security and covering the loans with treasury notes is not partisan. Bush borrowed 1.3 trillion and so did Obama. Theoretically the money will be paid in time for disbursements. Social Security is the largest holder of U.S. debt.

*"**America will be far safer if we reduce the chances of a terrorist attack in one of our cities than if we diminish the civil liberties of our own people.**" (Nancy Pelosi)*

According to Wolchover, Natalie, 2011, *Security in the United States has undergone a total overhaul since Sept. 11, 2001. You see it at airports, border crossings and even concerts. But there is no easy answer to whether the changes have made us safer.*

Those who think new safety protocols are working argue that the proof is in the pudding: Nothing like the 9/11 terrorist attacks have happened since. Others argue that hostility toward the U.S. has grown because of its post-9/11 policies and wars, making the threat of terrorism greater now than it was. Still others say that threat is (and always was) overblown, and that vast federal spending on counterterrorism has detracted from fighting ordinary crime, the real threat to safety.

Largely because of the Patriot Act, legislation signed into law by President George W. Bush on Oct. 26, 2001 (and extended by President Barack Obama), the FBI can now freely search emails, phone records and financial

The Patriot Act and The Freedom Act certainly take away from civil liberties. It is a potentially dangerous legislation that was meant to be a temporary means for our government to protect its citizens from future terrorist attacks. Obama did not have to re-enact the Patriot Act; he could have ended it. He chose not to do so. He had stretched the limits of the Act in order to conduct quasi-legal surveillance on U.S. citizens, including members of the Trump campaign.

According to Shear, Michael, 2015, *For more than six years, President Obama has directed his national security team to chase terrorists around the globe by scooping up vast amounts of telephone records with a program that was conceived and put in place by his predecessor after the Sept. 11, 2001, attacks.*

Now, after successfully badgering Congress into reauthorizing the program, with new safeguards the president says will protect privacy, Mr. Obama has left little question that he owns it.

The new surveillance program created by the USA Freedom Act will end more than a decade of bulk collection of telephone records by the National Security Agency. But it will make records already held by telephone companies available for broad searches by government officials with a court order.

"The reforms that have now been enacted are exactly the reforms the president called for over a year and a half ago," said Lisa Monaco, the president's top counterterrorism adviser. She called the bill the product of a "robust public debate" and said the White House was "gratified that the Senate finally passed it."

The president is trying to balance national security and civil liberties to put into practice the kind of equilibrium he has talked about since he was in the Senate, when he expressed support for surveillance programs but also vowed to rein in what he called government overreach.

Mr. Obama entered the Oval Office with what he called "a healthy skepticism" about the system of surveillance at his command. But Ms. Monaco said that, in part because of his often grim daily intelligence briefing, the president was also "very, very focused on the threats" to Americans.

The compromise on collections of telephone records may end up being too restrictive for the president's counterterrorism professionals, as some Republicans predict. Or, as others vehemently insisted in congressional debate during the past week, it may leave in place too much surveillance that can intrude on the lives of innocent Americans.

Either way, Mr. Obama's signature on the law late Tuesday night ensures that he will deliver to the next president a method of hunting for terrorist threats despite widespread privacy concerns that emerged after Edward J. Snowden, a former N.S.A.

contractor, revealed the existence of the telephone program.

"He owned it in 2009," said Michael V. Hayden, a former N.S.A. director under President George W. Bush, who oversaw the surveillance programs for years. "He just didn't want anyone to know he owned it."

Jameel Jaffer, the deputy legal director of the American Civil Liberties Union, called the USA Freedom Act "a step forward in some respects," but "a very small step forward." He said his organization would continue to demand that the president and Congress scale back other government surveillance programs.

In the case of the telephone program, Mr. Obama's preferred compromise was originally the brainchild of his N.S.A. officials, who embraced it as a way to satisfy the public's privacy concerns without losing the agency's ability to conduct surveillance more broadly.

In the lead-up to last week's congressional showdown, Mr. Obama and his national security team insisted that broad surveillance powers were vital to tracking terrorist threats, while admitting that the new *approach to data collection would not harm that effort.*

White House officials said Mr. Obama was comfortable that history would show that he struck the right balance.

"To the extent that we're talking about the president's legacy, I would suspect that that would be a logical conclusion from some historians," said Josh Earnest, the president's press secretary. Mr. Earnest said the compromise addressed anxiety about privacy but still gave the government access to needed records.

Mr. Obama's advocacy put him at the center of a fierce congressional debate over the surveillance program, which officially expired early Monday morning before lawmakers approved changes on Tuesday.

In the Senate, Senator Mitch McConnell of Kentucky, the majority leader, railed against the president's compromise proposal, saying, "We shouldn't be disarming unilaterally as our enemies grow more sophisticated and aggressive."

At the same time, Senator Rand Paul, Republican of Kentucky, excoriated Mr.

Obama, saying, "The President continues to conduct an illegal program," a reference to a recent ruling by a federal appeals court that the original N.S.A. telephone data collection program was not authorized by federal law.

What emerged from that debate was a rare bipartisan victory for the president, whose approach was met with approval by Republicans and Democrats in the House and Senate. Even some of the president's most ardent critics in the Republican Party endorsed the approach.

The compromise on the telephone collection program is part of a broader tug-and-pull for Mr. Obama, who inherited a vast national security infrastructure from Mr. Bush.

As a candidate in 2008, Mr. Obama was harshly critical of some of that infrastructure, pledging at the time to review every executive order by Mr. Bush "to determine which of those have undermined civil liberties, which are unconstitutional, and I will reverse them with the stroke of a pen."

Once in office, Mr. Obama did roll back some of Mr. Bush's decisions, in one of his first acts as president, he signed an executive order banning torture. But his national security team has also embraced some of Mr. Bush's methods, arguing that they are necessary to protect Americans against attacks and to fight threats abroad.

Mr. Obama talked about "putting careful constraints" on surveillance even before Mr. Snowden revealed the existence of the telephone program. Later that year, Mr. Obama explained how his thinking had evolved.

"I came in with a healthy skepticism about these programs," Mr. Obama said. "My team evaluated them. We scrubbed them thoroughly. We actually expanded some of the oversight, increased some of the safeguards. But my assessment and my team's assessment was that they help us prevent terrorist attacks. And the modest encroachments on the privacy that are involved in getting phone numbers or duration without a name attached and not looking at content, that on net, it was worth us doing."

With the passage of the USA Freedom Act nearly two years later, Mr. Obama must make his new approach work by maintaining a focus on security while doing more to respect privacy.

Nancy Pelosi voted for the USA Freedom Act. Nancy Pelosi voted for the Patriot Act in 2001 and against it is 2006. In speaking about the passage of the USA Freedom Act, Nancy Pelosi said the following.

"Congress has a responsibility to protect the security and liberty of the American people. Today, after the dangerous, unnecessary and avoidable lapse in authorization of national security tools, the Senate has finally passed the USA Freedom Act.

"The bipartisan USA Freedom Act overwhelmingly passed by the House provides thoughtful reforms of intelligence gathering tools designed to keep us safe. (Nancy Pelosi)

"I will not be making appointments to a committee that is not bipartisan." (Nancy Pelosi)

Of all the non-sensical things Nancy Pelosi has said, this one is truly makes no sense. Bipartisan means members of both parties on the same committee. Partisan means only the members of one party being on a committee.

If there is a committee of all Republicans, it is partisan. If Nancy Pelosi were to make an appointment, it would become bipartisan, but since she has said she will not do that, it would remain partisan.

If there is a committee of all Democrats, it is partisan, but Nancy Pelosi would have already made appointments to that committee. She has made no commitment to seeking Republican participation.

By holding true to her statement, Nancy Pelosi would actually be creating the situation she is vowing to avoid.

"My biggest fight has been between those who wanted to do something incremental and those who wanted to do something comprehensive. We won that fight, and once we kick through this door, there'll be more legislation to follow."
(Nancy Pelosi)

One of the biggest criticisms of Obamacare was that it involved too much changing at once. This is the comprehensive approach Mrs. Pelosi is speaking of. When things happen too quickly, they often fail because they were not well thought out before being implemented. Small changes allow time to evaluate processes, evaluate and adjust before the next changes come.

There was significant opposition to Obamacare and the democrats supporting the Act wanted to ensure it was implemented quickly and in full, fearing delay and reflection would cause it to disintegrate. Few people in congress even invested the time to read the lengthy. Pelosi obviously did not. Although she was the cheerleader for Obamacare, she could not even answer the most basic questions about it.

Making certain you are at the correct address, knocking on the door, opening it slowly, looking around, and then entering once safety was determined is a more effective approach than kicking in the door. Everyone involved in Healthcare were thrown into chaos. The American healthcare system which was respected throughout the world was distracted by over regulation and lost its ability to focus on excellent care.

According to Furchtgott-Ross, Diana, 2014, If the Affordable Care Act does not fail because of flaws in the law, it will likely be changed by Congress due to voter pressure. Already, the administration is delaying implementation of certain parts of the law because it is unworkable.

Implementation of the Affordable Care Act appears to have six major problems:

1. People are not signing up.

A new report shows that only 2.2 million people enrolled for plans in the exchanges in October through December, compared to a forecast of 7 million.

Of those 2.2 million, 24 percent were younger Americans aged between 18 and 34. The administration had forecast that 7 million people would sign up, and that 38 percent of them would be young people.

Without more customers, especially more young people, whose health costs are low, insurance companies will suffer losses that will be paid for by the federal government, raising the costs of the program.

2. Numbers of uninsured will remain high.

Even before the administration released its low enrollment figures, the Congressional Budget Office forecast that the Affordable Care Act was not going to achieve its goal of universal insurance.

3. Premiums are pricey.

One reason that people are not signing up is that premiums are higher than expected.

Paul Howard, Yevgeniy Feyman and Avik Roy of the Manhattan Institute found that Obamacare will increase underlying premiums by 41 percent, nationwide.

4. Deductibles are expensive.

For a bronze plan, the basic plan, deductibles can reach over $6,000 annually for singles and $12,700 for families.

That means that to access the plan's benefits, after preventive care, families have to spend $12,700.

5. People cannot keep their plans, despite President Obama's promises.

6. People cannot keep their doctors.

In order to keep costs down, insurance companies are reducing the numbers of doctors on their insurance plans, and eliminating some of the more expensive hospitals in the networks.

The basic problem is that Barack Obama promised his healthcare plan would benefit everybody. It doesn't. Under Obamacare, the government subsidizes the health coverage of some Americans while making it more expensive for others. People who have faced higher premiums, higher deductibles, and narrower choices of doctors know they're getting a bad deal.

"The Bible tells us in the Old Testament, 'To minister to the needs of God's creation is an act of worship. To ignore those needs is to dishonor the God who made us.' On this Earth Day, and every day, let us pledge to our children, and our children's children, that they will have clean air to breathe, clean water to drink, and the opportunity to experience the wonders of nature." *(Nancy Pelosi)*

Democrats have a pattern of rewriting history to suit their needs. It is far more difficult to do with a book, such as the bible, which others know well.

Pelosi's quotation sounded nice, but the Old Testament contains no such quote.

Thou shalst not misquoteth the Bible.

"This initiative is funded by the high end, we call it Astroturf It's not really a grassroots movement." (Nancy Pelosi)

Nancy Pelosi and the Tea Party do not like each other. In an effort to discredit her nemesis, she decided to raise questions as to the groups grassroots origins. She called it more like AstroTurf because the group had some corporate sponsorship.

The hypocrisy of course is that there are few if any liberal grassroot movements that are not corporate sponsored or sponsored by activist philanthropists such as George Soros.

According to Poor, Jeff, 2010, *It is patriotic to exercise the 1st Amendment by petitioning the government for a redress of grievances, unless of course your effort has a tie to some corporation or lobbying interest. Then regardless of its size, it's phony baloney Astroturf activism.*

While groups like the George Soros-funded MoveOn.org have managed to elude the "Astroturf" moniker, from its inception, the Tea Party movement has taken shots from its critics. One of the most popular left-wing charges was to call it "Astroturf," meaning it was presented as a grassroots effort, but wasn't really grassroots. Speaker of the House Nancy Pelosi labeled the Tea Party movement "Astroturf" back during the original Tax Day Tea Party protest on April 15, 2009.

"This initiative is funded by the high end, we call it Astroturf," Pelosi said. "It's not really a grassroots movement. It's Astroturf by some of the wealthiest people in America to keep the focus on tax cuts for the rich instead of for the great middle class."

That attitude has been widely echoed in media coverage of the Tea Party, as if it were a corporate effort to subvert the U.S. government's ability to collect revenue and redistribute wealth through public works and social program. Meanwhile, environmental causes, like Earth Day or global warming with their own corporate sponsorship - are rarely labeled Astroturf.

The Green Movement Openly Corporate Sponsored, But Never Labeled 'Astroturf' For many companies, environmental causes and saving the planet have become a clever way to market or advertise a product. It's a common phenomenon for retail outlets to use the environmental mantra to promote what they're selling. In fact, it's not only promoted by corporate interests, but it's something the federal government encourages businesses do to sell their product, according to the U.S. Small Business Association.

"If you are already competitive in terms of price, quality and performance, adding 'green' claims and eco-labels to your marketing strategy may enhance your brand image and secure your market share among the growing number of environmentally concerned consumers," the SBA Web site says. "Start your green marketing campaign by ensuring your green claims are credible. Do this by having your product certified that it was produced in an environmentally sound manner. Once certified, use the eco-labels from the certifying organizations to help consumers make educated choices."

And one has to look no further than Earth Day 2010 to see the corporate fingerprint on so-called green activist efforts. Major U.S. corporations like Proctor & Gamble, Siemens, Wells Fargo, AT&T, UPS, and Ford all had a major presence at the so-called Earth Day "Climate Rally" on the National Mall back on April 25. That's in addition to a sponsorship from NASA, a federal government entity and media outlets, including the Washington Post and Gannett's USA Today.

So, you have all the components - corporate interests and government bureaucracies collaborating to push a political agenda. Isn't that the textbook definition of "Astroturf?" Yet that label has failed to become a part of any green efforts.

But was that label ever applied by any media outlet to describe this particular Earth Day event? A Nexis search of the last 90 days reveals no media outlet has used the "Astroturf" marker for Earth Day.

And it goes much further than just a clever marketing gimmick or effort by big corporation to appease an activist movement. The leaders of the green movement are actually set to profit off of environmental policy. Global warming is lucrative, and regulations that would make carbon usage a commodity will profit some.

Speaker Pelosi and her ilk on Capitol Hill have had help from the media pushing the "Tea Party-as-Astroturf" idea. MSNBC's Rachel Maddow has regularly labeled it

Astroturf, disputing the movement's natural origins.

Despite the one-sided treatment of global warming and climate change in the media and a reluctance to call it "Astroturf," there is another perspective. Hundreds of scientists and policy professionals met in Chicago May 16-18 for the 2010 International Conference on Climate Change calling attention to dissent in the scientific community over assumptions that modern warming is man-made or that it is a crisis.

"I'm telling you, this is connected, it is no accident. It is a decision and it is as clear as can be. It's not only to monopolize his time, it's to undermine his name ... as he goes forward to protect and defend the Constitution of the United States." (Nancy Pelosi)

The Fast and the Furious was a scandal that took place under the Obama administration which directly involved Attorney General, Eric Holder.

According to Attkisson, Sharyl, 2014, *The general news media met the recent release of 42,000 pages of government documents, withheld for more than two years under President Obama's one and only invocation of executive privilege, with a predictable-yet-inexcusable yawn.*

The documents relate to the Justice Department case "Fast and Furious" in which federal agents secretly facilitated delivery of thousands of weapons to Mexican drug cartels.

The story was so significant that independent judges awarded it top investigative reporting honors two years straight. Yet many in the popular news media had declared it a political scandal of little consequence.

They'd bought into propaganda from government interests who used social media, bloggers and direct contact with news organizations to marginalize whistleblowers who exposed the wrongdoing, politicians who dared to ask tough questions and reporters who had the audacity to cover it.

Still, one would think the belated document release would generate widespread interest. After all, there's now an expressed consensus that the Obama administration has been the most difficult in recent times for press freedoms and transparency.

Ironically, it wasn't the press that forced release of the Fast and Furious material. It was private lawsuit by the conservative watchdog group Judicial Watch.

Review of thousands of pages revealed textbook examples of government attempts to manipulate the press.

Attorney General Eric Holder had given sworn testimony to Congress stating he'd only recently heard of Fast and Furious for the first time. But internal documents proved Holder's top aides had sent him briefings about the case many times the year before.

It's significant to note that in their email exchanges, the federal press agents weren't upset that the documents contradicted Holder's testimony. They were upset that I reported it. And they were also stumped as to why other journalists didn't publish articles even though that was their goal.

Matthew Miller, an outside adviser to Holder, suggested more ways to use the press for damage control. In an email, he writes Holder:

"...You could find a way to 'run into' a couple of reporters on your way to something. Maybe Pete Williams, Carrie, Pete Yost, that part can be managed. Most important is that you're in front of a camera in a relaxed manner giving a response you have rehearsed...It would be ideal if those two things happened in the same day so you didn't have two news cycles of responding, you want to do it all at once. There may be things you need to do to go on offense as well, but I think most important right now is that you answer the charge about covering this up. Then you can move to offense."

Pete Williams is an NBC News correspondent and Pete Yost reports for the Associated

Press. "Carrie" may refer to Carrie Johnson, who covered Fast and Furious for National Public Radio.

Other e-mails reveal a shocking claim on Holder's part: that he doesn't read his briefings from top aides. "Sigh," Holder writes in an e-mail about the briefings. "sure, I didn't read them. I rarely do."

It's hard to argue none of this is newsworthy. Additionally, it appears the e-mails should not have been withheld, as they do not appear to qualify for executive privilege. If the improper withholding of public information isn't challenged and punished, successors in either party have an implicit green light to repeat the offense. The press is allowing our constitutional freedoms and rights to be chipped away, with barely a whimper…rights that are easily lost but difficult to regain.

There was no connection to voter suppression, this investigation was about illegal arms being sold to drug cartel members, under the authority of the Attorney General of the United States.

According to Rosalsky, Greg, 2012, *Rep. Trey Gowdy called House Minority Leader Nancy Pelosi "mind-numbingly stupid" for suggesting that Republicans are attacking Attorney General Eric Holder in order to advance an agenda of voter suppression.*

"It's really beneath the office of a member of Congress to say something that outrageous, and the fact that she was once the Speaker is mind numbing," Gowdy told Fox News on Thursday. "So, I don't know what was wrong with her yesterday or today or whenever she said that, but I would schedule an appointment with my doctor if she thinks that we are doing this to suppress votes this fall. That is mind-numbingly stupid," he said.

Republicans are calling for Holder's head over the "Fast and Furious" gun-smuggling operation. The Department of Justice has invoked executive privilege, preventing certain documents from being released to the House Oversight Committee, which prompted the GOP-controlled committee to vote to hold Holder in contempt of Congress this week. Many top Republicans are also demanding his resignation.

But Pelosi thinks the anti-Holder drumbeat is about something else: Holder has pursued a series of anti-voter-suppression investigations in states around the country, including

Florida, where there are allegations of minority disenfranchisement.

Mrs. Pelosi is downplaying the significance of Operation Fast and Furious and the involvement of Eric Holder. It may be that she did not understand the significance of his role or it may be that she does understand but wants the matter to be swept under the carpet.

According to Reyes, Gerardo, and Santiago Wills, 2012, on January 30, 2010, a commando of at least 20 hit men parked themselves outside a birthday party of high school and college students in, Ciudad Juarez. Near midnight, the assassins, later identified as hired guns for the Mexican cartel La Linea, broke into a one-story house and opened fire on a gathering of nearly 60 teenagers. Outside, lookouts gunned down a screaming neighbor and several students who had managed to escape. Fourteen young men and women were killed, and 12 more were wounded before the hit men finally fled.

Indirectly, the United States government played a role in the massacre by supplying some of the firearms used by the cartel murderers. Three of the high caliber weapons fired that night were linked to a gun tracing operation run by the Bureau of Alcohol, Tobacco, Firearms and Explosives (ATF), according to a Mexican army document.

Univision News identified a total of 57 more previously unreported firearms that were bought by straw purchasers monitored by ATF during Operation Fast and Furious, and then recovered in Mexico in sites related to murders, kidnappings, and at least one other massacre.

As part of Operation Fast and Furious, ATF allowed 1,961 guns to "walk" out of the U.S. in an effort to identify the cartel leaders who received them. The agency eventually lost track of the weapons, and they ended up in the hands of Mexican hit men , including those who ordered and carried out the attack on a rehabilitation center in Ciudad Juarez where 18 young men were killed on September 2, 2009.

In Mexico, the timing of the operation coincided with an upsurge of violence in the war among the country's strongest cartels. In 2009, the northern Mexican states served as a battlefield for the Sinaloa and Juarez drug trafficking organizations, and as expansion territory for the increasingly powerful Zetas.

According to documents,175 weapons from Operation Fast and Furious armed warring factions across northern Mexico.

Many weapons cross the border and enter Mexico, but Operation Fast and Furious number, quantity and type of weapons had quite an impact in the war in this area.

Following the death of Border Patrol agent Brian Terry at the hands of Mexican bandits, media and Congressional investigations prompted hearings. In Washington, the Fast and Furious scandal became politicized, diverting the attention from the human cost in Mexico to political battles on Capitol Hill. In June, a vote to hold Attorney General Eric Holder in contempt ignored the real tragedy in Mexico.

Other firearms under ATF surveillance were permitted to leave the country from Texas, according to court documents and the exclusive testimony of Magdalena Avila Villalobos, the sister of an ICE agent who survived a confrontation with cartel hit men on a rural highway in Mexico. His fellow agent, Jaime Zapata, was killed during the attacks.

I support funding Planned Parenthood because I love babies. (Nancy Pelosi)

Democrats, in general, are strong supporters of Planned Parenthood. Planned Parenthood is politically active in its support of Democratic candidates because they rely on government funding. Many of us were shocked when Planned Parenthood committed to donate 20 million dollars to the Clinton election campaign. Had she won, her plan was to massively infuse Planned Parenthood with tax payer money to provide services worldwide. In reality, this was a money laundering scheme. The Clinton Foundation donated money to Planned Parenthood which was then donated to the Clinton Campaign.

Planned Parenthood claims that only 3% of their services involve abortion. These numbers are highly misleading. If during one visit a woman has a pap smear, pregnancy test, counseling, and contraceptives, she is counted into the numbers 4 times for that one visit. If she visits each month for her refill and receives the same basic services, she is counted into the number 48 times a year.

No matter how the numbers are counted or skewed, Planned Parenthood is the largest provider of abortion in our nation. It accounts for 35% of all abortions conducted in the country.

Planned Parenthood also targets black and Hispanic populations. 78% of their clinics are located in predominately minority neighborhoods.

According to Chapman, Michael, 2014, *In 2012, there were more black babies killed by abortion (31,328) in New York City than were born there (24,758), and the black children killed comprised 42.4% of the total number of abortions in the Big Apple, according to a report by the New York City Department of Health and Mental Hygiene.*

Those who believe the Democrats mantra that they are the party supporting minorities are being duped. By and large the democratic party supported slavery. The party was in fact created to oppose the abolition of slavery and were the founders of the Ku Klux Klan, which was originally created to attack Republicans. The irony of the current Democratic push to remove confederate statues is, that they were the people who installed them in the first place. Somehow Democrats manage to distract their followers by labeling Republicans as racist. Their followers rarely fact check history.

Margaret Sanger was the founder of planned parenthood. She was certainly not shy about her racist agenda.

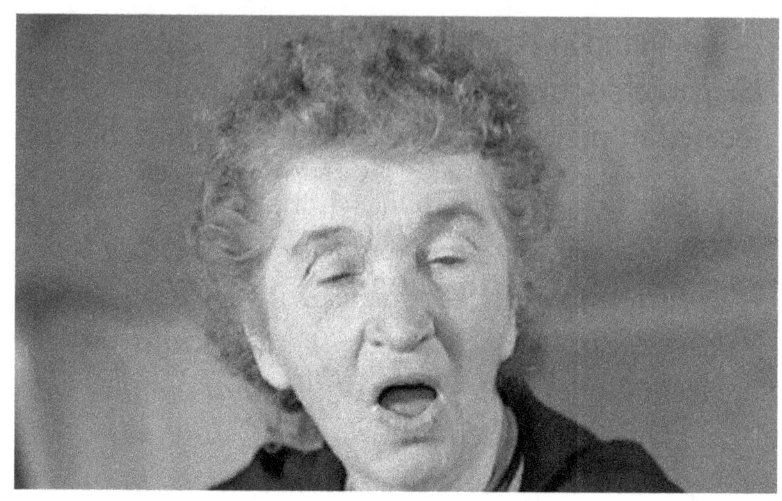

(Margaret Sanger)

Margaret Sanger has been lauded by some as a woman of valor, but a closer look reveals that Planned Parenthood's audacious founder had some unsavory things to say about matters of race, birth control, and abortion. An outspoken eugenicist herself, Sanger consistently promoted racist ideals with a contemptuous attitude. One rarely sees her quoted by Planned Parenthood leaders and apologists.

We should hire three or four colored ministers, preferably with social-service backgrounds, and with engaging personalities. The most successful educational approach to the Negro is through a religious appeal. We don't want the word to go out that we want to exterminate the Negro population, and the minister is the man who can straighten out that idea if it ever occurs to any of their more rebellious members. (Margaret Sanger)

This comment alone should be enough to understand the motives behind the founder of Planned Parenthood. She was deeming an entire race as being inferior and deserving of extermination. Her term extermination is also telling, since Planned Parenthood advocates are always touting the quality of life for the child as well as positioning their clinics in locations that provide easy access to minority populations.

The most merciful thing that the large family does to one of its infant members is to kill it. (Margaret Sanger)

Sanger argues that, because the conditions of large families tend to involve poverty and illness, it is better for everyone involved if a child's life is snuffed out before he or she has a chance to pose difficulties to its family.

We should apply a stern and rigid policy of sterilization and segregation to that grade of population whose progeny is tainted, or whose inheritance is such that objectionable traits may be transmitted to offspring. (Margaret Sanger)

Here Sanger was advocating forced sterilization of the part of the population she deemed to be inferior. She was also condemning the idea of interracial marriages or breeding. It's important to note that interracial marriage was illegal in the United States until 1967.

"Plan for Peace" from Birth Control Review (Margaret Sanger)

Article 1. The purpose of the American Baby Code shall be to provide for a better distribution of babies… and to protect society against the propagation and increase of the unfit.

Article 4. No woman shall have the legal right to bear a child, and no man shall have the right to become a father, without a permit…

Article 6. No permit for parenthood shall be valid for more than one birth.

Sanger's proposed baby codes were aimed at the poor who she felt required regulation of families. She was advocating for legislation that would punish people for having large families.

Along with the poor she was attacking Catholics and Mormons who tended to have large families.

Give dysgenic groups in our population their choice of segregation or sterilization. (Margaret Sanger)

Sanger has positioned herself to judge who is dysgenic and who is not. She already stated her target population.

Birth control must lead ultimately to a cleaner race. (Margaret Sanger)

The need to create a purer race was also a factor in Nazi Germany.

A woman's duty: To look the whole world in the face with a go-to-hell look in the eyes… to speak and act in defiance of convention. (Margaret Sanger)

(Sanger's, Go-To-Hell Look)

Nancy Pelosi's embrace of Planned Parenthood because she loves babies makes no sense when the truth behind the mission of Planned Parenthood is exposed.

As a pro-abortion Catholic, Pelosi has repeatedly come under fire for her voting record, including her opposition to the Partial-Birth Abortion Ban Act of 2003, and her long-term alliance with Planned Parenthood.

On receiving Planned Parenthood's highest honor, the Margaret Sanger Award, in January 2015, Ms. Pelosi said that she knew, "more about having babies than the pope", while affirming that a woman has "the right" to an abortion.

House Democratic Leader Nancy Pelosi had no interest in digging deeper into the revelations that the Planned Parenthood abortion business is selling the body parts of aborted babies. Instead, she wanted the Obama administration to investigate the pro-life activists who posed as undercover reporters to catch top Planned Parenthood doctors negotiating the sales.

"We have to confer with the Qataris, who have told me over and over again that Hamas is a humanitarian organization." (Nancy Pelosi)

Hamas is a Palestinian Sunni-Islamic fundamentalist organization. It has a social service wing and a military wing. Ignoring the military component does not mean it does not exist.

Ḥamas, is an acronym of Ḥarakat al-Muqāwamah al-Islāmiyyah, which translates in English to mean the Islamic Resistance Movement. The militant Palestinian Islamic movement in the West Bank and Gaza Strip is dedicated to the destruction of Israel and the creation of an Islamic state in Palestine. Founded in 1987, Ḥamas opposed the 1993 peace accords between Israel and the Palestine Liberation Organization.

Qatar has been a U.S. ally in the region. Despite their obvious support of terrorism, and the country being nick named the Club Med for terrorists, The U.S. government has been willing to look beyond this matter to focus on mutual goals. One of those goals is the overthrow of the Assad government and the building of a Qatari pipeline through Syria providing access to Mediterranean ports.

According to Blair, David & Spencer, Richard, 2014, *Few outsiders have noticed, but radical Islamists now control Libya's capital. These militias stormed Tripoli last month, forcing the official government to flee and hastening the country's collapse into a failed state.*

Moreover, the new overlords of Tripoli are allies of Ansar al-Sharia, a brutal jihadist movement suspected of killing America's then ambassador to Libya, Christopher Stevens, and of trying to murder his British counterpart, Sir Dominic Asquith.

Qatar, has dispatched cargo planes laden with weapons to the victorious Islamist coalition, styling itself "Libya Dawn". Western officials have tracked the Qatari arms flights as they land in the city of Misrata, about 100 miles east of Tripoli, where the Islamist militias have their stronghold. Even after the fall of the capital and the removal of Libya's government, Qatar is "still flying in weapons straight to Misrata airport", said a senior Western official.

The remarkable truth is that few in the Middle East would be shocked. From Hamas in the Gaza Strip to radical armed movements in Syria, Qatar's status as a prime sponsor of violent Islamists, including groups linked to al-Qaeda, is clear to diplomats and experts.

Qatar's promotion of extremism has so infuriated its neighbors that Saudi Arabia, Bahrain and the United Arab Emirates all chose to withdraw their ambassadors from the country.

Take Syria, where Qatar has been sponsoring the rebellion against Bashar al-Assad's regime. In itself, that policy places Qatar alongside the leading Western powers and much of the Arab world.

But Qatar has deliberately channeled guns and cash towards Islamist rebels, notably a group styling itself Ahrar al-Sham, or "Free Men of Syria". Only last week, Khalid al-Attiyah, the Qatari foreign minister, praised this movement as "purely" Syrian.

Far from being a force for moderation, Ahrar al-Sham played a key role in transforming the anti-Assad revolt into an Islamist uprising. Its men fought alongside Jabhat al-Nusra, an al-Qaeda affiliate, during the battle for Aleppo and they were accused of at least one sectarian massacre.

Instead of fighting Isil, Ahrar al-Sham helped the jihadists to run Raqqa, the town in eastern Syria that is now the capital of the self-proclaimed "Caliphate".

Last December, the US Treasury designated a Qatari academic and businessman, Abdul Rahman al-Nuaimi, as a "global terrorist". The US accused him of sending nearly £366,000 to "al-Qaeda's representative in Syria", named as Abu Khalid al-Suri.

Mr Nuaimi is also accused by the US treasury of transferring as much as $2 million per month to "al-Qaeda in Iraq" and $250,000 to al-Shabaab, the movement's affiliate in Somalia. Mr Nuaimi denies the allegations, saying they are motivated by his own criticism of US policy.

Critics question why Qatar has failed to act against him. It's deeply concerning that these individuals, where sufficient evidence is in place to justify their inclusion on the US sanctions list, continue to be free to undertake their business dealings.

In the case of Syria, Qatar's chosen method for supporting its favored insurgents is to pass large sums to middlemen in Turkey. These figures then use the money to buy weapons from third countries, notably Croatia, and arrange for their onward transfer to rebels in Syria. Experts question how much control Qatar has over this process and whether the middlemen might be pursuing their own aims and pocketing much of the money. Qatar was handling weapons and supplies for Syria, but they were never really keeping a full grip on the nature of the conflict.

Qatar has let Hamas, the armed Palestinian movement, base its political leadership in Doha since 2012. Qatar's government has funded Hamas and the previous Emir paid an official visit to the Hamas-ruled Gaza Strip in 2012.

As a small country with relatively weak armed forces and 250,000 citizens, Qatar is trying to guarantee its security by reaching in every direction. As well as providing an office for Hamas, Qatar also hosts the forward headquarters of US Central Command and the al-Udeid military airbase, serving as the hub for all American air operations in the region.

As a member of congress, we should expect that those entrusted to protect and defend the Constitution actually know the contents and meaning of the Constitution. The First Amendment encompasses the Freedom of Speech, Freedom of Religion, Freedom of the Press, Right to Peaceably Assemble and the Right to Petition the Government for Redress. The Second Amendment encompasses the Right to Bear Arms.

The Second Amendment has nothing to do with hunting or recreation. The Second Amendment encompasses the Right of the People to keep and bear arms. As scary as it may be for today's congress, the Right to Bear Arms was designed to allow the people the ability to overthrow the government if it were to become tyrannical.

"Firearms stand next in importance to the constitution itself. They are the American people's liberty teeth and keystone under

independence ... from the hour the Pilgrims landed to the present day, events, occurrences and tendencies prove that to ensure peace security and happiness, the rifle and pistol are equally indispensable ... the very atmosphere of firearms anywhere restrains evil interference — they deserve a place of honor with all that's good." (George Washington)

"I ask, Sir, what is the militia? It is the whole people. To disarm the people is the best and most effectual way to enslave them." (George Mason; Co-author of the Second Amendment)

"The supposed quietude of a good man allures the ruffian; while on the other hand arms, like laws, discourage and keep the invader and plunderer in awe, and preserve order in the world as property. The same balance would be preserved were all the world destitute of arms, for all would be alike; but since some will not, others dare not lay them aside ... Horrid mischief would ensue were the law-abiding deprived of the use of them." (Thomas Paine)

"Are we at last brought to such humiliating and debasing degradation, that we cannot be

trusted with arms for our defense? Where is the difference between having our arms in possession and under our direction and having them under the management of Congress? If our defense be the real object of having those arms, in whose hands can they be trusted with more propriety, or equal safety to us, as in our own hands?" (Patrick Henry)

"Those who hammer their guns into plowshares will plow for those who do not." (Thomas Jefferson)

"The best we can help for concerning the people at large is that they be properly armed." (Alexander Hamilton)

"What country can preserve its liberties if their rulers are not warned from time to time that their people preserve the spirit of resistance. Let them take arms." (Thomas Jefferson)

Pelosi praised the 23 executive orders issued by Obama and endorsed his call to reinstate the 1994 "assault weapons" ban, implement a universal background check system and institute a ban on magazines holding more than 10 rounds.

She has been one of the first to jump on the gun control bandwagon whenever there is a national tragedy or domestic terrorist attack. Democrats tend to politicize gun tragedies even though there is no way to regulate weapons of those who are using them for illegal purposes. Gun control only takes rights away from responsible gun owners.

On November 8, 2005, San Francisco voters enacted Proposition H, a total ban on the manufacture, sale, transfer or distribution of firearms or ammunition in San Francisco, as well as a ban on the possession of handguns within the city by San Francisco residents.

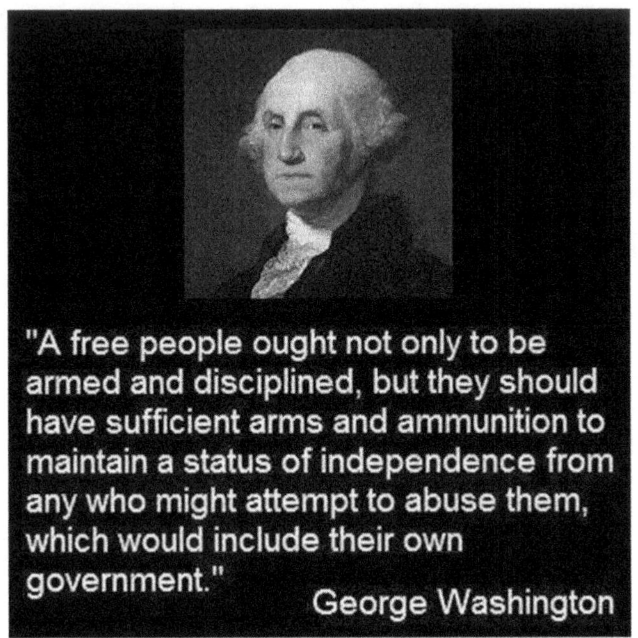

Bibliography

Adams, Mike. "Global Warming Data FAKED by
    Government to Fit Climate Change
    Fictions." NaturalNews, 2014

Attkisson, Sharyl. "How Eric Holder Spun the
    'Fast and Furious' Scandal to a Lapdog
    Media." New York Post, New York Post, 14
    Dec. 2014

Blair, David, and Spencer, Richard. "How Qatar Is
    Funding the Rise of Islamist Extremists."
    The Telegraph, Telegraph Media Group, 20
    Sept. 2014

Chapman, Michael. "NYC: More Black Babies
    Killed by Abortion Than Born." CNS News,
    20 Feb. 2014

Crawford, Phillip. "FBI Files: Congresswoman
    Nancy Pelosi's Father Thomas D'Alesandro
    Jr. Was 'Constant Companion' Of Notorious
    Mobster Benjamin Magliano." Friends of
    Ours, 2015

DeSilver, Drew. "5 Facts about Social Security."
    Pew Research Center, 18 Aug. 2015

Furchtgott-Ross, Diane. "Six Major Hurdles to
    Implementing ObamaCare." National Center
    for Policy Analysis, 2014

Hayward, John. "Climate-Change Advocates
    Collect Big Money from Interested Parties."
    Breitbart, Breitbart News Network, 8 May
    2015

Lucas, Fred. "Pelosi Won't Divest Drug Stock,
    Dismisses Conflict Claim." CNS News, 7
    July 2008,

Malkin, Michelle. "Pelosi and the Treasure Island
    Land Grab." MichelleMalkin.com, 18 Aug.
    2010

Markay, Lachlan. "Corruption from Democrat
    Nancy Pelosi: Once AGAIN, Her Husband
    Benefits." Right Thinking, 2014

Markay, Lachlan. "Pelosi's Husband Invested in
    Solar Firm Weeks Before Expansion."
    Washington Free Beacon, 19 Apr. 2016

McClanahan, Carolyn. "People Don't Hate
    Obamacare, They Hate the Cost. Fix That
    GOP." Forbes, Forbes Magazine, 3 May
    2017

Newsmax. "'60 Minutes' Uncovers Pelosi's Insider
    Stock Trades." Newsmax Inc., 13 Nov. 2011

Poor, Jeff. "The Media's Untold Story of Astroturf:
    Corporate Sponsored Environmentalism."
    NewsBusters, 2010

Potter, Wendell. "Elimination of 'Public Option' Threw Consumers to the Insurance Wolves." Center for Public Integrity, 16 Feb. 2015

Reyes, Gerardo, and Santiago Wills. "Fast and Furious Scandal: New Details Emerge on How the U.S. Government Armed Mexican Drug Cartels." ABC News, ABC News Network, 30 Sept. 2012

Rucker, Phillip. "As Democrats Lose House, Nancy Pelosi's Historic Reign as Speaker Ends." The Washington Post, WP Company, 3 Nov. 2010

Sanchez, Ray. "Exclusive: Speaker Nancy Pelosi Says She Has 'No Regrets'." ABC News, ABC News Network, 3 Nov. 2010

Seidl, John. "Pelosi: 'We Haven't Really Gotten the Credit for What We Have Done.'" TheBlaze, TheBlaze, 25 Oct. 2010

Shear, Michael D. "In Pushing for Revised Surveillance Program, Obama Strikes His Own Balance." The New York Times, The New York Times, 3 June 2015

Thorn, Victor. "Pelosi's Trail of Corruption." American Free Press, 2010

Wolchover, Natalie. "Are We Safer Today than on 9/11?" LiveScience, Purch, 6 Sept. 2011

World Biography, Nancy Pelosi, 2017